I0463112

Everything You Need to Know in Selling

You Learned in Youth Sports

By
Tryst Marlowe Anderson

Table of Contents:

This book is dedicated to all of the youth sport coaches who change the lives of their players by building character, persistence,ethics and sportsmanship.

Introduction

Millions of people were first introduced to competition through youth baseball, pee wee football, youth soccer, YMCA basketball or possibly a church athletic program. Although those activities were fun and provided exercise, the most important lessons they taught us were associated with character building, teamwork, and the cost of winning. Legendary Basketball coach, Bobby Knight once said, "Preparing to win is more important than winning." Preparation is the cost every athlete pays in order to win. Youth sport coaches begin this process for their players.

Sun Tsu, the legendary Chinese general had this to say in The Art of War, "Victorious warriors win first and then go to war, while defeated warriors go to war first and then seek to win." Was he talking about victors being prepared while defeated warriors simply go to battle?

The unsung heroes in building the leaders of tomorrow are youth sport coaches. Character development is the key ingredient of the sport participation process for young people. Do professionals only need character to be successful?

Not by any stretch of the imagination. Key, important and integral should not be confused with only.

It is like having only one shoe or dressing for success without any pants. Therefore, it is the synergy of all of this book's chapters that mold a successful sales career. Character building is part of a larger process.

In an ideal environment, this book would analyze all youth sports. There would be repetition and redundancy as the key principles related to sales' careers would be documented again and again. Therefore, this book will focus on baseball. Baseball is the great American pastime.

This is not just about boys developing into men. Youth baseball offers many opportunities for girls to learn these skills as well. In fact, girls' softball is growing in significant numbers throughout the country. In other words, this book examines life skills that are not sexist.

Baseball is a game of winners and losers. Everywhere from the one league town to the Little League World Series, scores are kept.

In the politically correct world where branding winners at the expense of losers is not tolerated, Little League baseball has continued to grow. Other youth sports try to keep scores from being known during the actual games. However, participants always know what the score is. In fact, many youth soccer leagues allow a team being beaten by more than 4 goals to put an extra player on the field. This extra player certainly doesn't represent the red badge of courage.

Some parents believe keeping score will scar their children for life and look at sports as being only about fun and exercise.

They are correct about the fun and exercise, but miss the boat when thinking that sports can't teach their children life lessons. A few school districts have even experimented with changing the way teachers grade students in order to protect their feelings. Psychologists will tell you that it is important to help children learn about the rules of achievement early in life. It is all part of the process of setting boundaries, accepting responsibility and living with accountability.

Since score is kept in life, the life lessons of youth sports are certainly worth learning. And, nowhere is score more important than in the life of a professional salesperson.

That is the beauty of youth baseball. It doesn't just simply teach boys and girls that score is kept and one team wins while another loses. It prepares them to do something about it. It teaches them to be proactive instead of reactive. How many successful sales people are reactive?

Even when a team is down by five runs in the bottom of the sixth inning, the home team has its rally caps on. The cheering gets louder. The players continue to play hard until the last out.

This book shines a light on youth baseball specifically and youth sport coaches in general that illuminates the world of professional sales. Wait until you get to the chapter where closing is discussed. You won't believe the powerful tools youth sports have given to people to be successful at closing the sale. Every peak performer will want to evaluate the basics of this book and understand where their baseline for success was generated. Parents will want to read this book to understand the powerful life lessons that are being taught to their children when they participate in youth sports.

In addition, every parent's organization will want to provide copies of this book to every coach in their leagues and thank them for the investment they are making in the lives of their players.

So get ready to find out what youth baseball has to do with sales success!

Fundamentals start early in youth sports.

Chapter 1—FUNDAMENTALS:

Taking Your Sales Career Back to Basics

Imagine you are eight or nine years old and sitting in the car with your mom, dad or both your parents on your way to try out for youth baseball. You have never played organized sports. Your father kept you out of "T" ball because he didn't believe that was really the way baseball should be played. He was wrong.

When your friends questioned why you didn't play, your father would tell you there was plenty of time for you to learn the fundamentals when you were old enough for the minor leagues. Your friends would later tell you that your father was crazy. He would often take time after work to play catch and hit balls to you. You also played on baseball fields with your friends and picked teams from the kids who showed up to play.

Now the time has come to actually become part of a team. You enter the field where the registration and try outs are being held and stand next to your father, who gets in line to sign you up. It is a very busy place.

A couple of your friends, who have been playing "T" ball, are joking around with some other boys. They are already part of the club.

When you reach the front of the line, your father is questioned about whether you have played "T" ball. Before he could answer another parent, who appeared to have some authority in that place, tells the registrar "I know him and his son. He is ready for the minor leagues." With that vote of confidence, the registration process proceeded.

On this day, before the first ball was thrown or hit, the young man learned a valuable lesson. If you are not part of the club, it is good to know someone who is. Beyond knowing them, they need to believe in you. In your sales career has this ever helped you get into a new account? When you were not part of the "club" did you find someone with credibility to open the door to an eventual sale?

In sales, the tools of the trade are often taken for granted. How many times have we heard companies and sales organizations claim they need to "get back to basics"? The basics really are the fundamentals. In the same way that government can't tax itself out of a recession; you can't "hi-tech" your organization back to the fundamentals.

There is no way to paint over a lack of fundamentals to make sales or service shine again. If the corporate culture shifts from client service to simply delivery of services or products, you can't Twitter your way back. The fundamentals must be introduced again just like the youth sports coach does at the first practice. There are no shortcuts to proficiency in sport or sales.

The coach begins like this: "I know all of you think you know how to play baseball and that it is as easy as swinging a bat and throwing a ball. Today, I want to introduce you to the equipment, how to take care of it and what you need to do to make it work for you." From those introductory words begins the baseball journey. The fundamentals of the game are the same for everyone, but coaches will teach them differently. That doesn't change the fundamentals. You may have learned the fundamentals of sales in one industry and now work in another. Did the fundamentals of the sales process transfer to the new industry? A company can't move forward until a customer is found. Sales brings in customers.

Whether you sell a commodity or service, or whether there is a long lead sales cycle or short, the fundamentals of the sales process are the same. Why else are there so many generic "back to basics" sales courses?

It is because the fundamentals stay the same, but sometimes we need to be reminded that a strong foundation is required to be successful in building a profitable sales career.

Hitting and fielding are the two primary areas where fundamentals must be taught beginning on day one. Pitching is another fundamental area that will come into play within a few days. In other words, even laying out the fundamentals is a process. Do you think baseball put the fun in fundamentals? Not hardly!

The boys and girls, getting their first taste of this organized sport, only want to play the game like they have on the playgrounds when they choose up sides. It is not part of their DNA to appreciate an hour of fielding ground balls or chasing balls in the outfield during batting practice.

What about the players who enter this arena with limited athletic ability? In the Chapter 7 you will learn why every player on the roster gets a chance to play. Therefore, those who need help with the fundamentals get it. They are also told to repeat the drills when they are at home. Repetition is the key to learning any new skill. How many of you still remember the multiplication tables you learned in grade school?

You remember because you had hours of repetition using flash cards until they were burned into your memory. How many of you remember the game you played immediately after your multiplication table home work was finished?

This is true in the sales profession as well. The idea that some people are born for sales should be considered an urban myth. If an outgoing personality is the fundamental criteria for success in sales, then why are so many introverts successful? Limited skill sets at the beginning of a sales career does not doom the person to failure.

If the person is willing to work, learn and model the characteristics of successful sales professionals, they can achieve anything in their career.

The fundamentals apply to every position on the field. This is the same as in sales. Every sales manual or training program contains the fundamentals of the sales process. At its core, it is the same for high ticket items as it is for professional services sales. The exciting thing about youth baseball is the stepping stone sequencing of fundamentals to fun with "da mentals". Baseball is a mental game that must be fun. Professional baseball players are often quoted about how they would be doing this even if they weren't being paid.

In other words, the game is still fun for them. However, when you are starting out, it is difficult to understand how the work will eventually be transformed into fun.

The youngsters go from registration with parents to the field where a strange adult starts teaching them how to catch, throw and hit. When their brains begin to process the repetitive actions in those early practices, they realize that the fun of the game will increase as they become better at the fundamentals. Yes, baseball is still mostly a mental game.

Batting practice is a great example. In the beginning, the coach lobs the ball across the plate and it is easy to hit the ball. Confidence builds among even the least talented players. In a few weeks the pitchers on the team will be throwing batting practice, or the coach will start throwing faster. However, the early success has prepared the players for the faster pitching ahead. When you began in sales did your mentor put you through the same kind of process or was it a baptism by fire? Your experience might have been a lot like mine.

I started with an engineering firm and was responsible for sales in the Midwest.

My only previous sales experience was as a newspaper carrier when I was 10. The newspaper was actually delivered for free with advertising inserts.

However, in order to make extra money, I had to try and collect money from people who were supposedly receiving a free newspaper. For three years I made money delivering these newspapers. At the age of 27, with experience as a marketing director for a national trade association, I was hired to sell engineering services that I wasn't familiar with to clients I didn't know. To say the training program lacked the process found in Little League is an understatement.

The Vice President of Marketing gave me this advice to start me on my journey of professional sales. "Know where our offices are located and the names of our officers and office managers. Review these project photos (he handed me a dozen photos with project descriptions on the back) and you will do fine." This was my introduction to sales and my only sales training program. Is your story similar?

I was with this firm for 12 years and rose in the organization to become the Chairman of the Corporate Marketing Committee.

In addition, I was in charge of conducting sales training programs for chief engineers, marketing managers and new offices as they were opened. The Midwest Region led the company in sales for 10 of the 12 years while I was with the firm. My initiative even got me involved managing planning studies where my client list exceeded 25.

Does this mean that training isn't a prerequisite for sales success? If that were the case, then youth sports would be a chaotic collection of teams picking up sides and arguing over who got to bat first. Training brings order and direction to the process.

It also means that in the absence of effective training, the person needs the initiative to obtain the knowledge needed to be a peak performer. It worked for me. Personal initiative only goes so far and I would recommend training for everyone. In fact, over the years, I have participated in a number of training and education programs geared to sales effectiveness, communications, client service, and marketing.

Every sales person should have some kind of education activity on their "to do" list. Peak performers are always evolving and improving their skill sets.

This is especially important in the new economy. By the way, I was also a youth baseball player for four years.

Many youth players will purchase training aids in DVD format, go to batting cages and practice with their parents to extend the training they receive from coaches. Players learn the importance of training.

All players don't have equal potential. Michael Jordan would have been a good basketball player, if he didn't practice. However, he became the greatest basketball player in history because of his passion for practicing to become the best. It is this passion for training that is transferred from youth coaches to the children on their teams that will make the difference when they become adults.

One thing that training won't help you with is rejection. Counseling might help. "Rejection" is not on the agenda of any sales training programs. Nobody wants to see the big "L" flashed in front of them. When someone rejects you're your feel like a loser. However, people in the sales profession are constantly subjected to rejection. Some leave the profession because of it. Most simply develop thick skins and learn to use it to their advantage.

If properly applied, rejection can be a great motivator for future success. It helps young players as well.

Overcoming rejection is critical for success in sales. It is like a blister on your foot. At first it hurts, but properly treated, a callous will develop. The next time the skin receives the same rough treatment, it won't blister.

Peak performers don't blister over rejection. The experience of youth baseball is one reason why. After all, the world's best baseball players hit the ball safely only three times out of ten. Very few pitchers have recorded 27 strikeouts in a game. There is a lot of opportunity for rejection in baseball. The sooner you learn to deal with it, the sooner you can move on and not be bothered by it.

Sales professionals look forward to it because they understand that without a certain amount of rejection; they won't have the opportunity to use their fundamental skills to close the sale.

Young baseball players learn this lesson in the first weeks of the season. They can't throw the ball far and their hitting is atrocious. But, their arms get stronger and they throw with greater accuracy. Their eyes and hands work together to make contact with the ball.

Rejection is always scratching at the door. They feel the sting of rejection each time they strike out, make an error or their team loses. Every blister heals and the game is still fun.

Accurately throwing a ball is another fundamental of baseball. Although some are natural throwers, techniques can enable even those with weak arms to have great performances at certain positions.

Speaking of natural, don't we all identify with "natural" sales people? They have the gift of gab and can sell ice cubes to Eskimos. Yet, even the "natural" sales person becomes better when skilled in the fundamentals of the art of sales.

As mentioned previously, even an introvert can be successful at sales when the person becomes a student of the fundamentals.

Not every baseball player has to be able to hit home plate with a strike from deep center field. But, they have to reach the cut-off man. In teaching youth the fundamentals of baseball, coaches show them how to build on their strengths.

Often in sales, we are told to work on our weaknesses. Where does that leave us?

What are your weak performance areas and are they associated with the fundamentals? If you spend a certain amount of time improving weaknesses, what does that do with your overall performance? It probably makes you average.

However, if you concentrate on improving your strengths, you will become superstars instead of average sales people with few weaknesses. This is especially true if your weaknesses are not key to your career success. For example, my office is always a mess. This has always been one of my weaknesses. I could spend some time to clean the office or attend a seminar on the value of a clean office, but what would either of those do for my sales performance.

If my sales didn't hit quota, would the manager tell me during my review that the bonus was still mine because I had the cleanest office in the company? Time is our most precious resource. Therefore, spend your time improving your strengths and you will see a huge return on your effort.

Baseball teaches that there is room for strong arms and weak arms, but they need to be put in the right position in order to be successful. Is everyone in your organization in the right position?

Hitting: Making Contact with the Ball

Eye and hand coordination are essential for being a good hitter. What skills do sales people need to make contact with customers and clients?

Like hitting a baseball, multiple skills must be coordinated to close a sale. Some people are gifted in this area and always seem to bring the right skills together to match the current business opportunity. Have you ever considered the circus juggler a "multi-tasker" or just a performer? When you handle multiple tasks aren't you a lot like the circus juggler. What happens if everything doesn't stay up in the air?

This brings us to the multiple tasks a young person takes on when entering the batter's box. Can the fundamentals help a good hitter? Fundamentals keep the hitter sharp in the batter's box. There might be a player on base. The hitter has to check with the coach for a signal and also concentrate on the pitcher. Once the ball is released, the hitter has to make an instant decision whether it is worth hitting. Sometimes he swings only if the coach has told him to swing. All of these things are going on in his mind and the fundamentals keep him focused. In addition, the opposing team is yelling for him to swing and fans are screaming his name.

Controlling fear in the batter's box is a critical hitting fundamental that a coach has to instill in the heart of his players. That is why the coach lobs the balls in at first. Eye and hand coordination doesn't work when your eyes are closed. There is a battle going on between the pitcher and the catcher. The coach has to teach his players how to win the battle. After fear is removed, the player can stand comfortable in the box and challenge the pitcher to throw him a good pitch.

Fear is also a factor is sales. This is especially true when you are trying to move an engineer or other technical person into sales. Whenever you take someone out of their comfort zone, they experience fear.

How do you help them overcome their fear of the sales process? First, never give them the "baptism by fire" and send them out to sell without any preparation. They are like the first time baseball players who need the coach to lob the ball to them until they build confidence. So, how do you build confidence without sending them out on their own? I call it baby steps. Maybe you start with phone calls. You might want to schedule a lunch with a potential client and bring him along. After all it is only lunch! We all need to eat.

Yet, as the conversation over lunch proceeds, you can get the technical person involved in the conversation. When you debrief after the lunch, you ask the person what he thought of the encounter. Then you tell him that is what an initial sales presentation is all about.

It begins with a conversation, evolves into a discussion of what they need and ends, hopefully, with the client confirming the need for another meeting. This is about a relationship. It is like starting a conversation with your neighbor.

Then you can tell the "new sales person" that the next meeting is on him. Be prepared to give him some appropriate reading material related to sales, as well as material on the client company. Make time to meet with the person again before the next meeting to mentor and give affirmation of his ability to connect with the client.

This is the process that has worked for me in helping technical staff begin to overcome the fear of making contact with potential clients. In fact, I have developed a four-hour presentation on how to help technical people become effective sales representatives.
The next chapter also contains information on what you should do with technical people and others who are new to sales.

Practice will keep you from riding the pine.

Practice is not something that young players embrace. This is particularly difficult when they see professionals like Alan Iverson making a career out of missing practice. However, the coach schedules a practice every day in order to build the skills the players need to be successful.

Sometimes a coach has to resort to incentives to get his players to show up for practice. Peer pressure from team mates is the best method. However, with complex family schedules getting in the way of practice time, youth sports coaches have a more difficult challenge today than when I played the game over thirty years ago. In retrospect, it was probably just as difficult for players to make the decision back then because we were totally responsible for riding our bicycles to the practice. If you played before the advent of "soccer moms" then you understand what I am talking about.

Practice teaches players a lot more than the skills needed to be successful in youth sports. It also shows them that there is a price to be paid to improve. The price includes time and delaying pleasure. They must make a decision not to do something that might be more enjoyable at the time.

There were many practice days when my bicycle almost parked itself in the public swimming pool parking lot because of the summer heat.

Practice guarantees that repetitive behavior will improve performance on game day. Practice also improves attitudes.

When you have a presentation before a big client, do you wing it? Do you take what you have presented to the last client and re-package it for today's presentation? Successful sales people plan and practice every presentation. Although they might not concentrate on the sales skills, they do go over the client's needs, the value of their solution and rehearse answers to possible objections. When game day arrives for them, they are ready for the battle. They are at once the pitcher and the batter. Their practice has prepared them for switching roles. Good sales people don't get flustered if they strike out in the first inning and don't get too excited when they hit a home run to start the game. Their success is geared to finishing the game a winner. This is also another area where you can help your technical people prepare for sales and lessen their fear. Let them sit in on a few rehearsals to see how the process works and learn how to identify client needs. The rehearsal is the time to focus the team on their role.

If mistakes are made, be sure to engage in constructive criticism. Encourage your team to raise the bar on their performance.

Speaking of rehearsals, do you always scout the room where your presentation will be held? Unlike baseball, where the dimensions of the field are the same, meeting rooms are not. The best presentation in the world will fizzle, if the room does not conform to your needs.

The coach speaking to his player after a strike out uses encouragement. He teaches that there is more to the game than one out in one inning. He also teaches that a bad attitude from a small failure will compound itself and that could hurt the team. Do you use his words in your rehearsals or sales strategies today?

The Coach inspires players to work as a team.

Teamwork is probably the common denominator of what a coach teaches players in any youth sport. Teamwork is certainly essential in any team sport as it will be later in life.

Pitchers rule in baseball and young pitchers can become arrogant about their abilities. The same is true in the world of the professional sales person. Sometimes the good ones think sales success is all about them and they forget about the team. They forget that everyone from the receptionist to the clerk in the mail room play a role in their success. Who is on your team? Is there room for the "Golden Rule" in your organization? I am not talking about who has the gold makes the rules, but about doing to others what you would like them to do for you.

Therefore, the first item of business for a youth sports coach is creating a team concept for youngsters who have only experienced the playground. Since some of the players have never been chosen for teams during recess at school, this is an exciting concept. For the pitchers or otherwise talented athletes, it isn't as good because the show is no longer just about them.

The coach begins by explaining the importance of every position. The significance of the first and third base coaches and the use of a cutoff man when throwing into the infield are just two examples of teamwork he might use. Pitchers learn about the value of their catcher. The team concept hits home when they are reminded that a double play doesn't happen because the pitcher struck a batter out. Yet, the coach doesn't diminish the role of the pitcher by teaching the importance of teamwork. He explains that every part has a function. Some positions are more important than others at particular times of the game. Therefore, teamwork is about focus and being prepared to play your role when called upon to perform. Players learn that they can rely on the other team members to perform their role as well.

What do players not on the field do when their friends are playing on the field? When an opposing player comes to the plate, they start chanting, "Hey batter, hey batter, swwwwiiiiiinng batter" every time their pitcher throws the ball. They also encourage the teammates on the field as they will be encouraged (Golden Rule) when they take their positions later in the game or in the next game.

They learn that the team is more than just the players on the field at any particular time. As members of the team, they have to maintain focus on what is happening on the field.

The most important teaching about team performance is that the team is like a family. Families only encourage their members and don't demean them. Families stick up for their members and help them. When a family member does something wrong, good families encourage them to do better the next time.

This isn't about white washing poor performance.
It is about developing the concept of teamwork among a group of youngsters who have never played on a team. The coach alone is in charge of dealing with attitudes and behaviors that detract from peak team performance.

With this in mind, do you believe you will have a new appreciation for your team? Will you help them when you can and rely on them to perform their roles in making your sales efforts a success?

Does the pitcher control positioning?

Anyone involved in sales understands positioning. The company marketing helps some with a prospect's understanding of your products or services. But how do you really position your firm in the prospect's mind to effectively sell anything?

Could youth sports have taught you anything about positioning that will be beneficial as you try to enter the prospect's mind and world? To completely understand the coach's dilemma, you need to think back to your first sand lot baseball games. Remember when you did the ritual with the baseball bat to determine who would get the first pick? Then you would go through the collection of kids who had assembled on that field to play the game. One-by-one you pick players, with the "captain" of the opposition alternating with you. If there weren't nine players for each team, concessions were made. There was no tryout to determine who would pitch or play a particular position.

The players knew who the pitcher should be and right field was the place for the weakest player.

34

This was usually the last person chosen. The game began after the final selection and there were no coaches. Outfielders stood beyond the infield in a place of their choosing. Sometimes the captain might tell them to back up, if a particularly good hitter came to the plate.

The infield played where they were comfortable playing. Positioning was not important to them. They only wanted to play, get three outs on the other team and have their turn to bat.

Things changed when they entered the world of Youth sports. Positioning mattered! Right field was an important position when left handed batters came to the plate. With runners on base, the infield had to focus on how they were positioned to make retire hitters when a ball would be hit to them. If a ball was hit to center field and a runner was on second base, where would the shortstop go after the hit? Could he get to the cutoff position quicker, if he was closer to second base? The coach knew how to position the team for success.

Baseball was no longer nine players randomly scattered across a field in hopes that they would be near the action. Now the coach had a plan to give the players a higher probability of being near the action.

Positioning is another lifelong learning experience coaches transfer to youth baseball players.

There are multiple ways to position your firm in the mind of the prospect and client. You want your name to be the first thing the prospect thinks of when a need for your product or service arises. Learning the concept that a systematic approach will be more beneficial than a random collection of strategies wasn't taught to salespeople at Wharton. It was delivered to you by a youth sports coach who was showing you the benefit of playing your position in helping the team win. You would no sooner have a scattered positioning plan than you would eliminate your current CRM system. However, if you aren't constantly updating your CRM data, you are creating a scattered positioning system by default. In addition, remember that positioning is not just about you and the client, or your firm and the client. It is about you, your firm and your team; and the client. In today's economy and sales cycle, it could also be about client and client. Do your existing clients help you position your firm with other clients and prospects? Have you created a mechanism for getting them to talk with each other? Is there a better way to increase sales opportunities than to have two existing clients talking to each other about the superior service you deliver? This will help you sell more!

The coach delivers a simple life lesson that might be about baseball.

5—COACH: The Person Behind the Success in Sales

In the Strategic Sales Training programs I have developed over the years, a coach is one of the most important people in the sales process. You might refer to this person as a mentor or champion, but whatever the name, we all need at least one in order to succeed in sales. Why is a coach necessary for proven sales professionals?

When you know or identify the people who will influence the selection of your services, a coach is needed to help you walk through the selection process. You need to know who has the most influence, are funds available, is your product or service needed, when the decision will be made, what is the risk and is it safe to make the next move. These questions are all part of an effective sales strategy. They apply to whether you sell wigets or design services. Your coach has to have credibility with the client and with you.

How could a youth sports coach bring benefits to or model this process? The coach has taken your game from the sandlot to real organized baseball. Secrets you never knew about the game are also revealed through the coach.

He also speaks words about living that your parents or friends never told you about.

For example, the use of profanity was popular among the boys I grew up with. It changed one day when our coach heard a player use the wrong word. Instead of berating my friend, he simply said that the use of profanity is a sign of someone with a limited vocabulary. If you want people to think you are smart, don't use profanity. None of the players ever spoke a profane word at practice or games after that speech. Nobody wants their friends to think they are stupid.

For a baseball example, did you ever try to bunt when playing with friends on the sandlot? Bunting is a strategy that only a coach could reveal. The coach also teaches you signals to indicate whether you should swing, take a ball or bunt. As a player you begin to learn the value of the batting order and why certain players perform better at specific locations.

Finally, you learn about the coaches at first and third base. In youth baseball, these are usually players who are not in the game at the time. As a player you learn the importance of being a base coach. You hold in your hands another player's ability to score, remain safe or be called out. In reality you can be the difference between winning and losing.

You learn the inherent power of the coach. You also learn the batting signals and can transfer them from the coach to the batter. You are the eyes for the runner moving from second base after a hit to the outfield. He relies on you and your hand movements to tell him to keep running and head for home or to wait at third. He will also tell you whether the play will be close at third and get you prepared to slide. The base coach turns out to be the next best thing to being in the game. Students of the game are great base coaches because they take what the coach is telling them seriously. Have you ever seen a base coach who might not have taken his coach's training seriously? Just look for the runners who are regularly called out at third for one indication.

Our coaches in the sales arena do the same thing for us. Learning the value of coaches in youth baseball helps us appreciate the value that coaches will bring to our sales career. Coaches are important behind the scenes assets for improving our chances of success in any business opportunity. As a sales professional you need to constantly cultivate coaches because at least one is needed for every sales opportunity you pursue. If your career doesn't include coaches, you are playing in the sandlot and giving your competition a strategic advantage.

The rules apply to everyone equally.

We all must live by rules. Sometimes it seems that our competitors don't play by the rules. What do the rules of youth sports have to do with anyone's prospects for a career in sales? If you have ever heard of the saying, "level playing field", you know the reasons why youth sports rules are an important foundation for future sales success. In Little League baseball there are 60 feet between bases and the distance from the pitcher's mound to home plate is 46 feet. Everyone has to run the same distance between bases. Pitchers all throw the same distance. There are no deviations in the rules related to a player's size or athletic ability. Taller players technically don't have to throw as far or use as many steps to reach the base. The strike zone is reduced for smaller players. The rules establish the base line for team performance. It is not as if someone with a weak arm can walk up ten feet closer to home plate to begin pitching.

All industries have base lines as to how sales are performed. Some would call this a code of ethics or code of conduct. Despite the AIG and Bernie Madoff scandals, most companies are ethical and operate with a code of conduct.

Design firms operate under a code of professional conduct, as do other professional industries, like accountants and lawyers.

Would you ever see this on a mission statement published on a corporate website: "We will be ethical some of the time. When it is in our best interest, we will bend the rules." Not likely is it? Some would say this comes from the values of our Founding Fathers. If you look at the first set of rules, "The Ten Commandments", you can see how these have long-lasting impact. Yet, human nature is such that sometimes people try to improvise. This is especially true in the dog-eat-dog world of sales.

Rules are not just for naïve suckers who finish last. For many of us, they began in youth sports.

Here is a review of some other Little League rules. Designated coaching boxes are located at first and third base. The maximum bat length is thirty-three (33) inches and maximum barrel diameter may not exceed 2 1/4 inches. Beginning in 2009 all Youth sports bats must be labeled with a Bat Performance Factor (BPF) of 1.15 or lower. The upper limit of the strike zone extends to the batter's armpits.
A batter is out after the third strike regardless of whether the pitched ball is held by the catcher.

Sometimes rules evolve because someone figured out a way to get around the rules. This is what happened with the bat rule in youth baseball.

Often it goes to an interpretation of a vague rule. Yet, we are nothing, if not for our rules, or in the greater sense laws.

Pitchers in all divisions are limited to a specific pitch count per game and a mandatory rest period between outings. These vary with age and the rest period also depends on the number of pitches thrown. A base runner may not leave their occupied base from the time-of-pitch until the pitch reaches the batter. Therefore, there is flexibility in some rules.

If a fielder is waiting at the base with the ball, an advancing runner must attempt to avoid contact. A runner may not slide head-first except when retreating to a previously held base.

Every player on the team roster must have at least one plate appearance and play six consecutive outs on defense in each game. The penalty for a manager violating the rule is a two-game suspension.

Some coaches, not just youth sports coaches, believe rules are made to be broken.

There are countless examples in college and professional sports. When young boys and girls first learn the game, this is the worst kind of coach they can have. Rules bring stability to the game. Those coaches who live on the outer edge of the rules usually bring other baggage with them to coaching.

They become the "poster coaches" of what not to do and, more often than not, are the ones who face suspension some time in their coaching career. Therefore, this book is not about celebrating the exceptions to upholding the rules, but rather to the exceptional and dedicated coaches who build character while following and enforcing the rules.

Some rules are meant to be interpreted. For example, the strike zone is part of the rules. However, it is the umpire who enforces the rule. As long as the umpire is consistent, neither team will argue. The same is true for close plays at any of the bases. In youth sports, the best coaches teach their teams that the umpires/referees are human and can make mistakes. With that being said, they let them know that the umpire's decision is final and they need to respect the umpires. Do you respect the "umpires" in your profession?

Your umpires come from a variety of places. Sometimes they are your peers in allied organizations like SMPS. They might be staff members of organizations like APPA, SCUP, CoreNet, IFMA, ASHE, AAAE, IPI, etc. Why would you consider a staff person in the category of umpire? These are organizations where marketers of professional services will find clients. It is also where others will find customers. The staff can open doors for your business development efforts. Do you need a better location for your exhibit? Maybe you need advice on how to make a presentation to the members? Or, you want to have an article published in their monthly trade magazine. Staff regulates, just like a baseball umpire, the activities of the trade association and its members. You need to respect them and make them look good, or you will never get the "call" you need to make progress with their members.

Winners always have the smiles on their faces and they shake the opponent's hand.

How often did you hear as a child learning the game that "winning and losing wasn't important, but how you played the game was?" Vince Lombardi, the legendary football coach is often misquoted with this statement, "Winning isn't everything, it is the only thing." What he actually said was, "Winning isn't everything, but the will to win is everything." He also had this statement that applies to youth sports where parents don't want to keep score, "If it doesn't matter who wins or loses, then why do they keep score?" Whether the scoreboard lists the score or not, the players know who is winning. Why try to hide it. Winning and losing is an important part of character development.

Every time you pick up teams for any game, you know there will be an outcome. One side will walk away the winner. You might not care if it is your team as long as you had fun doing it. Joining an organized sport like youth baseball doesn't remove the joy of simply playing the game; it expands the joy to recognize the power of team play. Practice and improved performance is measured in the win column.

But, you say, what about the teams that go an entire season without a victory? First, how could they have enjoyed the game as losers? Second, how can this experience prepare them for careers in sales?

For the players who quit the team, the experience didn't do much to prepare for them for a career in sales. But, for the others who accepted the risk of peer ridicule, cat calls and the humiliation of being associated with a team that loses every game, their lives are better because of the path they travelled. Remember the thick skins needed for sales professionals? These young players might have even seen opposing coaches bend the rules and wonder about the fairness of their predicament. If they were blessed with a good coach, they would have learned one of our most important lessons as sales professionals, "Life isn't fair." This isn't a retreat from life and declaration that they are victims. It is really important that children learn that bad things happen to good people and good things happen to bad people.

In baseball it is one's preparation that helps to control the outcome. Therefore, the time spent at team practice and the time dads spend helping their children with the fundamentals all work together to build the character that is needed to survive an 0-for-the-season experience.

Children also need to learn there will be another day and another season. This isn't a childish false hope. After all, the Chicago Cubs have been living this reality for the last 100 years and are still waiting for a World Series Championship.

Sales is a tough business where personal defeat happens more often that soaring success. It is a career where rejection is expected on a daily basis.

What childhood experience could be better preparation for this than a losing season with a youth sports team? It is not a lonely experience because you have shared it with your team. Obviously, the emotional impact of such an event is directly related to the character of the coach.

What about the teams that win the championships? Even those teams with a .500 season have developed in the players the foundation for life success. This translates directly to sales success. Since few teams will go through a season undefeated, the team and players have learned the importance of focus, detail, perseverance and dedication. They have experienced a positive return on their investment of time to become ball players and received the dividend of growing character that will last a lifetime.

They have also experienced, as Jim McKay coined, "the agony of defeat."

In many ways, even players on an undefeated team have experienced the pain of losing every time they strike out, are called out or make an error in the field. Obviously, these personal losses are less traumatic than losing all of your games as a team. But, there are lessons to be learned in any failure. In fact, the whole notion of sportsmanship revolves around an athlete's ability to handle the pressure of winning and losing. Have you ever seen a sore winner? Probably not, but you have seen winners who snub the other team. This is not what sportsmanship is about. Most youth sport coaches require their team to shake the hands of their opponents after every game. They must do this whether they win or lose. It is what sportsmanship is all about. Coaches are the first to teach players how to be humble in victory and graceful in defeat.

When the Chicago Bulls were on the way to their first NBA Championship, they had to defeat the Detroit Pistons to reach the finals. When they finally reached the summit, what did Detroit do? They walked off the court without as much as a hand shake. Isaiah Thomas, their All Star point guard, led the way.

It was embarrassing to the league and the Bulls. Chicago didn't act that way the previous two years when Detroit beat them to go on to win the title. Beyond the league embarrassment was the message this display sent to young people just learning the game. Even when professional sports players believe they are not role models, they are. This is just another reason why youth sport coaches are so important

Why is the ball thrown around between innings?

8—WARM UP: Peak Performers Always Warm Up

Many youth baseball teams begin working out indoors in January. Why do they do this and what does it teach the players? In order to be ready for the season, they have to get their arms in shape. They have to start easy and work up to full speed. In addition, they have to get their eyes ready to see the ball so batting practice is part of the warm up regime.

The life lesson is to understand the importance of preparation in putting yourself in position for peak performance.

When the season starts, warm ups are part of every practice and every game. Players learn that you can't just show up a few minutes before the umpire yells, "Play ball" and expect to be a peak performer. Even these young bodies need to learn the benefits of stretching, moving, throwing and swinging before they take the field for real. They learn that the time the infield and outfield take between innings to throw the ball is important on a number of levels. This warm up that takes place every inning brings focus back to each position. It is both a mental and physical exercise.

Is a warm up part of your routine as a professional sales person? There is a lot to be said about the mental aspect of warming up before a sales call or client presentation. But, what about the physical? Do you do any physical warm ups before sales calls or presentations? If you remember the value physical warm up had on your performance as a youth baseball player, you will take another look at physical warm ups before you make your next big presentation. The primary benefit of a physical warm up is that is releases built up energy and the adrenalin associated with any performance. Remember, a warm up is just that, a few exercises to get you ready to perform. When going through baby steps with your technical staff or anyone new to sales, you might want to emphasize the presentation warm up regime. People who are more likely to be nervous before a presentation are best served by simple exercises that help relieve pent up energy and adrenalin.

I am not talking about a complete physical work out prior to your sales call or presentation. A few stretches and maybe some jumping jacks as you leave your car and walk to the meeting. Depending upon your distance in the parking lot, you might simply walk a little faster as you head toward the building. If you have been riding in your car for more than 30 minutes, these exercises are even more important.

Don't stagnate while you wait in the reception area. You can do an easy warm up with your hands.

Simply bring your hands close and curl your fingers together. Then pull outward for ten seconds as an isometric exercise. Wait about thirty seconds and repeat. If you are nervous about the presentation, do some simple breathing exercises before the meeting. Breathe in slowly through your nose counting to 10. Then exhale through your mouth while counting to ten. Do this twice before you are called into the meeting. Think of your ideal vacation experience as you exhale and your nervousness will be left in the reception area. In a Lamaze class this would be called taking a "cleansing breath." I call it taking a selling breath.

Warm ups are an essential part of learning to be a youth sports player. The concept of the warm up is also extended to preparing your mind and body for a peak performance. What are the key points you plan to make at the presentation. Have you committed these to flash cards that you go over prior to the meeting? This is different to the complete rehearsal. It is just getting your mind ready for the performance. It is taking away the clutter that has been part of your day prior to the meeting. It is returning your mind to focus on the mission.

It is why your youth baseball coach was adamant about taking practice throws around the infield and outfield between every inning.

The physical act was not intended to improve your performance. It was intended to be a mental exercise to help you regain focus on your mission in the field. Your coach didn't want you to waste your mind between innings of the baseball game. He wanted you to be ready.

A few years ago the Negro College Fund had an advertising tag line, "A mind is a terrible thing to waste." There is a lot of truth to this statement.

You shouldn't waste your mind as you prepare for the presentation or sales call. Knowing every word and crossing every "T" is not what I am talking about. The warm up exercises are about clearing your mind. As a peak performer, you are already prepared to do your best. You just don't need to have brain clutter get in the way of your powerful performance. Some of the brain clearing is accomplished through the physical exercises.

Think about this the next time you are arriving at a sales call or presentation.

If you are part of a team for the presentation, let them in on your secret. Let them know about this during the rehearsal, especially if you have inexperienced project people on the team. Let them know that this is what peak performers do to stay on top of their game.

The player knows the situation and where to throw the ball.

A good coach takes his players through situation exercises during practice. He will set up a runner on base and tell the fielders how many outs they have. Then he will hit the ball to a specific position and wait for the reaction. If the correct play is not run, he will remind the players of the correct play. Then he will change the conditions and hit the ball again. He will continue to do this to recreate actual game situations that his players must be prepared to deal with.

For example, what happens in a run down with another runner on base?

The coach will also run situations for when his team is batting. What do runners do with one out versus two outs? He works these situations with the players who also serve as base coaches. If a player has to think about what to do with the ball when it is hit to him, the player is less likely to make the correct decision or, in his haste to do something, throw the ball away. Situation practice takes away the anxiety of fielding a ball during game conditions.

Do you practice situation planning as a sales professional? When you rehearse your presentation do you simply go through the points of the presentation and make sure all the participants say the right thing? If that is all you do, you are missing the point of rehearsal. Someone has to serve as the client. Someone has to see the presentation from the client's point of view. Lawyers do this all the time in preparing for trial. Presidential candidates do this when preparing for debates. Your rehearsal has to present client situations. What if the client asks us this question? What if they ask us about the lawsuit we settled last year? What if the selection committee changes and a new economic buyer is sitting at the table. What if……….. You fill in the blank.

In the same way the youth baseball coach worked to create the environment for his players to have their best performance, so it is with you. Peak performance during a presentation will come to a quick end, if the client surprises you with questions or changes you didn't anticipate. The fact that you have prepared for changes in advance changes the mindset of your presentation team as well. They enter the room prepared for something to change. Do you know the most important "what if" to prepare for? What do you do, if the computer freezes or the projector stops working? Does your team know what Plan B is?

The coach prepared the players for this situation. Have you prepared your team?

Persistence means running out every hit.

There are many examples of persistence in youth baseball and youth sports in general. The one thing that defines persistence at any level of baseball is beating out a grounder. If it isn't the first push toward persistence, it is right near the top. The coach has to instill in the players that when the ball is hit, you run as hard as you can to first. It doesn't matter whether you think it is a blooper to the pitcher or a fly to the outfield. You have to run to first on every pitch. Why is this persistence so important? Sometimes the infielders make errors. Sometimes the blooper takes a weird hop and gets to the outfield. Sometimes balls are dropped in the outfield. Sometimes pitchers overthrow first base. Persistence in baseball is about the sometimes working in your favor.

Of course there is the character of persistence in practice and showing up for games. Some players with lesser skills than others have gotten into games because of their persistence in practice. A coach will give more weight to a player who knows the game and has practiced, than a great athlete who hasn't practiced or doesn't know the game.

You have to have persistence to keep coming back when there are other distractions in your life. You have to have persistence to keep coming back when others tell you that you are not good enough. Persistence is developed by a coach who affirms his players not just for their abilities, but also for their attitudes.

Is persistence part of your character as a peak performer in the sales industry? Every great sales person has had to develop persistence along with the thick skin required to achieve success. The "can't take no for an answer" is the hallmark of every sales person worth their salt. But, sometimes we get worn down and tired of the pursuit. We begin to listen to the naysayers who tell us all the reasons why a particular firm will not buy from us. Do you ever get to the point of giving up?

What do you think Abraham Lincoln would say about giving up after personal failure? As a young man, Abraham Lincoln went to war a captain and returned a private. Afterwards, he was a failure as a businessman. As a lawyer in Springfield, he was too temperamental and impractical to be a success. He tried politics and was defeated in his first try for the legislature. He was defeated again in his first attempt to be nominated for the United States Congress.

65

He tried to be Commissioner of the General Land Office and lost. The senatorial election of 1854 brought him another defeat. He tried to be selected Vice President in the 1856 election and lost, and was defeated in the senatorial election of 1858.

At about that time, he wrote in a letter to a friend, "I am now the most miserable man living. If what I feel were equally distributed to the whole human family, there would not be one cheerful face on the earth." Yet, Abraham Lincoln is considered by many the greatest President the United States has ever had. What if he would have stopped reaching for his dream after the first couple of election losses? What if he hadn't run hard to first base after he hit the ball?

I have had many experiences where an extra effort to a reluctant prospect meant success. There is a great story in the Bible about persistence.

The disciples had fished until dawn without success when Jesus appeared to them on the shore. You can imagine their attitude at that point in time. They wanted to pull up their nets and join Jesus on the shore. Then Jesus yells from the shore, "Try the other side of the boat."

You can imagine their lack of enthusiasm after a long night of fruitless labor. But they followed the command and their nets nearly burst with the catch.

Selling is a lot like that experience. Often it is just one more call that brings success. I remember a prospect for a relatively large project that made me a lifetime believer in persistence.

We were asked to propose on a project worth $500,000 in design fees. We were not close to the prospect, so I began the due diligence process. The client was a large county outside of Chicago. Their suburban campus had exploded and they needed to build a large parking structure for a new courthouse building. Six firms were invited to submit qualifications. At the time I was working for the largest firm in the world that specialized in parking planning and the design of parking structures. The qualification submittal went off without a hitch. A few weeks later, we were asked to submit a proposal. I continued to contact the list of buying influences, started calling architects who had designed other buildings on the campus and researched the county's hot buttons for pursuing this project. I found out that the County Executive was not taking appointments.

After the proposals were submitted, three firms were invited to an interview. So far, I had only been doing what every salesperson would do by making sure all of the bases were covered.

We went to the interview, focused on the county's needs and made a great presentation. This would be the first structured parking facility on the campus. While most of the buying influences on the selection committee asked good questions, the economic buyer did not. The County Executive was the economic buyer. Not only didn't he ask a question, but he never changed his expression during the entire interview.

Nothing happened for weeks after the interview.

My follow up activities revealed that a principal for one of the firms was also the chief fund raiser for the Republican Party in the county and a close friend of the County Executive. You have all been faced with a "wired" competitor and know how this can affect the best strategy. We finally received a phone call telling us that we had given a thorough presentation, but no decision had been made. In fact, we later learned the project was on hold. Who wants to kiss their sister when they are pursuing a $500,000 project?

This is where the opportunity got interesting and my persistence went into high gear. Since the "wired" firm hadn't been awarded the project, there was a chance that we were still a viable contender. Our only question was when would we get our second chance?

I started a guerilla marketing campaign that went to both the elected commissioners, as well as the other buying influences. In addition, we were working for the municipality where the county campus was located, so we had a coach who kept us up-to-date on what was happening with the county.

Finally, about a year after our first interview, we were called in for a second interview. This time there would be only two firms under consideration. The other firm was the "wired" competitor. What could we add to this presentation that we didn't present the first time? Should we bring the same team? Do we have a chance? Some of the principals thought we were chasing a ghost and wasting our time with another presentation.

I thought differently. Modifications were made and a rendering of our proposed solution was created. If the interview were held today, we would have created a movie depicting the rendered parking structure along with visually showing how someone would navigate through the interlocking floors. That technology wasn't available at the time.

The president of our firm was added to the presentation team. We entered the meeting room full of hope and confidence. The County Executive hadn't changed from the first interview. However, he did look over at the rendering several times. He didn't ask questions or thank us for taking the time to make the second presentation.

After the presentation, I followed up with all of the buying influences, including the County Executive. Except for the County Executive, they all believed we had blown away the other firm. But, the County Executive would make the decision.

A week later we were awarded the project. Since the county had delayed the decision for so long, they had developed another parking crisis on their campus. Shortly after we were awarded the first parking structure, we negotiated the design fee for a second parking structure.

Persistence was able to generate close to $1 million in revenue for our firm.

About a month later we had to make a presentation to the municipality.

The project manager was having coffee in a diner shortly before the meeting was scheduled to start when a member of the county selection committee, a county commissioner who was part of my contact plan, went over to his table. He asked whether we knew why we were selected. If the project manager was an arrogant type, he could have answered, "Because we are the best firm in the country." Instead he acknowledged that he didn't know.

"You were hired because your rendering had a brick façade," was his short answer. He said the other firm used precast concrete spandrel panels on their rendering. The County Executive's office looked out on the site of the new parking structure. His building was clad in brick. In making his selection, the County Executive told the other members of the selection committee, "If they (the "wired" firm) don't even know that my parking structure needs to have brick, what else don't they know about parking structures?" The "wired" firm had made it all the way to a second presentation with the experience of only one parking structure in their portfolio.

In one sense this case study is an example of the power of client loyalty. Yet, it also proves that client loyalty can only go so far. However, it also shows the bigger example of how persistence can change a no into a yes.

From that point on I have never been dismayed by a slow response from a client who is in the process of making a selection. I always want to run hard to first base after I hit the ball.

In fact, there have even been some instances where another firm was told they had a contract (not yet signed) and the firm I was working for ended up receiving the award. The old adage, "It's not over until the fat lady sings,' is certainly a word to the wise for building up your persistence in pursuing a client. Persistence should have its limitations. A salesperson can only spend so much time chasing a project that might be a ghost.

You need to look at the fee associated with the immediate project, as well as the potential lifetime value of the client. If both of these are on the positive side of the chart, then you should spend as much energy as it takes to win the job.

There are many examples of persistence in sports and many are great stories for motivating salespeople to go the extra mile. I will offer one. The United States Men's Soccer team participated in the 2009 FIFA Confederations Cup in South Africa, the site of the 2010 World Cup. The team lost to Italy by a goal and was blasted by Brazil 3-0. They defeated Egypt 3-0 to advance to the semi-finals against Spain.

Spain was the number one team in the world, had not allowed a goal in the Cup, and had not been defeated in some 35 matches. After losing to Brazil, everyone had written off the US team. Some pundits were writing that the Americans lacked "heart".

A victory over Egypt did not assure them of advancing to the semi-finals. They had to have scored more goals than Italy. Persistence and focus on the task at hand landed them in the semi-finals where they defeated the unbeaten Spanish team 2-0. The persistence continued to the championship game against Brazil. They didn't have a happy ever after ending, but they did take a 2-0 lead in the first half, Brazil came back in the second half to win by one goal.

However, this did not make the United States Men's Soccer team losers.

Think back to their loss a week earlier to the same team by the score of 3-0. They came back with persistence.

This is the kind of persistence that our youth sports coaches gave us as youngsters and give our children today. It is also the kind of persistence that every peak performer in sales needs to be a success.

They don't teach you persistence in college or make it part of the curriculum when pursuing your MBA. Persistence is really a mainstay in the school of hard knocks. I believe these words of Jane Adams say it the best, "Nothing could be worse than the fear that one had given up too soon, and left one unexpended effort that might have saved the world."

In our daily endeavors whether it be pursuing our profession, hobbies or family, the amount of persistence is directly proportional to the outcome of our efforts.

I blocked for a future NFL Hall of Fame player.

EPILOGUE

Throughout this book you have seen the tangible life learning experiences that youth sport coaches have given to children. These gifts span beyond the physical fitness value of participating in sports.

Applying this to peak sales performers is a view of youth sports that has never been explored. The idea that youth sports coaches have helped mold the character, attitude and performance of millions of young people in the United States and around the world has a powerful connection to anyone involved in sales. Whether you sell professional services like architecture, accounting and engineering, or sell physical products, the connection between youth sports and your career is important.

What are the key success factors for anyone involved in selling? Can you be a peak performer, if you don't have a coach, lack a sales account strategy, aren't persistent, dislike your team, or never practice? Then the connection to your youth sports experience makes sense.

If you didn't participate in youth sports and you are still a success in sales, more power to you! You learned the lessons in some other place, perhaps from your parents or other mentors.

Maybe you are just starting a career in sales and you are looking for an edge. You are looking for the practical steps you need to take to become a peak performer. Like any profession, you haven't started your career with the hopes of being mediocre. Therefore, you search out training opportunities and written material to help you close sales. Your success is easy document. Either you close sales, or you don't. Therefore, training and education are important elements to your success strategy. This book was written to help peak performers return to their roots and bring advice to novice sales people to look at where they have come from. You might have even had a special coach in your youth who brought more to your life than the lessons I have documented in this book. Youth sport coaches in general give players more life lessons than have been documented in this book. After all, I didn't even touch on handling a "hot temper" or temper trantrums, but youth coaches live in that world.

The purpose of this book was to highlight 10 lessons that contribute to the success of anyone in a sales career.

If you have children in youth sports or about to begin youth sports keep in mind that they will be learning more than the basics of the sport and receiving more than the physical training associated with the activity.

Your children will be at the start of lessons that will stay with them for the rest of their lives. The ultimate value of these lessons will be directly related to character of the coach.

You might want to re-read Chapter 5 to understand the importance of the coach's character.

Finally, I want to acknowledge all of the youth sport coaches who influenced my life. Everyone from Mr. Fisher at the YMCA to the pee wee football and baseball coaches who took time out of their lives to change the lives of players who were assigned to their team.

When I was the offensive right tackle on the pee wee football team, Elgin Tigers, I protected a quarterback named Dave Casper (yes, the Hall of Fame Tight End with the Oakland Raiders). Coach Zeller mentored me to keep working for the next season when Dave would be too old for the team.

He was a coach, who knew I was being raised by my grandparents and took time to reveal a level of understanding I only now can appreciate.

In baseball I had excellent coaches who took a hot-headed, less talented brother (my older brother was a great baseball player) and helped him learn the value of being part of a team. They helped the "lefty" understand why shortstop would never be his position.

You might be like me and millions of others who didn't appreciate the ultimate value of their youth coaches and now will understand that to one degree or another, our ultimate success can be tracked to those early days on the sports field when those life lessons seemed like hard work and interaction with outsiders really began.

In a culture of deteriorating values, lack of personal commitment to anything and selfish attitudes, it is time to recognize the value of our youth sport coaches.

I have to quote Sun Tsu from the Art of War once again, "Can you imagine what I would do, if I could do all I can?" Coaches not only do all they can, but in doing that they make their players the best they can be. Tom Peters says this effort is "Doing God's work."

Coaches, I thank you for your service to the youth of America. God bless you!

www.ingramcontent.com/pod-product-compliance
Lightning Source LLC
Chambersburg PA
CBHW072041190526
45165CB00018B/1304

* 9 7 8 1 4 4 8 6 3 3 6 9 2 *